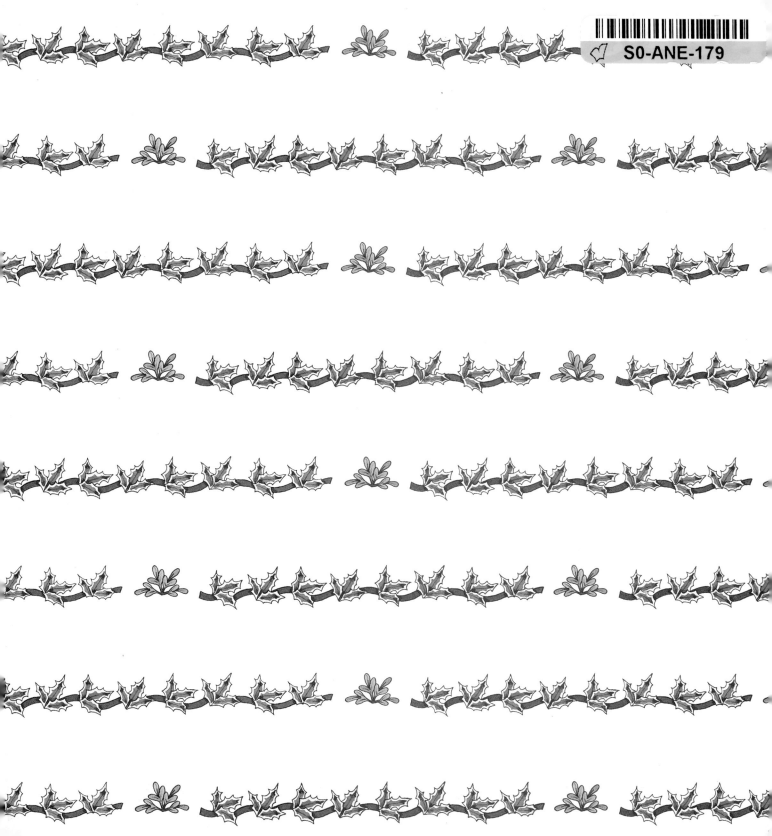

Lights and Music of Christmas

Deck the Halls

Illustrations by Kathleen O'Malley

PUBLICATIONS
INTERNATIONAL,
LTD.

$\mathcal{D}$eck the halls
with boughs of holly!
Fa la la la la la la la.

'Tis the season
to be jolly,
Fa la la la la la la la.

Don we now
       our gay apparel,
Fa la la la la la la la la.

Troll the ancient
       Yuletide carol,
Fa la la la la la la la la.

_S_ee the blazing Yule
before us,
Fa la la la la la la la.

Strike the harp
 and join the chorus,
Fa la la la la la la la.

$\mathcal{F}$ollow me
  in merry measure,
Fa la la la la la la la la.

While I tell
  of Yuletide treasure,
Fa la la la la la la la la.

*F*ast away
      the old year passes,
Fa la la la la la la la la.

Hail the new,
      ye lads and lasses,
Fa la la la la la la la la.

*S*ing we joyous all together,
Fa la la la la la la la.

Heedless of the wind
and weather,
Fa la la la la la la la.